6 Keys to a Last
Volu
– A Resource for Making it Work

Barb's "6 Keys" Book Series

Book 1

6 Keys to a Lasting Relationship:
Volume 1
– A Resource for Making it Work

6 Keys to a Lasting Relationship:
Volume 1
– A Resource for Making it Work

Book Title & Author

6 Keys to a Lasting Relationship:
Volume 1
– A Resource for Making it Work

By

Barbara Waller-Johnson, BS, MA, MFT

6 Keys to a Lasting Relationship:
Volume 1
– A Resource for Making it Work

Copyright & ISBN

Publisher: Self-Published
ISBN: 978-1-7347456-0-3

6 Keys to a Lasting Relationship: Volume 1 – A Resource for Making it Work

DEDICATED TO:

My husband Big Wil, with whom I have been blessed to share a long-lasting and loving relationship with, for 47 years to date. Thanks for showing me the world from a different vantage point.

My mom Mary and dad Rev. Stephen, who were blessed to share 63 years of marriage that ended only when dad was called home to be with God, and mom being reunited with him 16 years later.

All my clients that came seeking answers to their relationship issues and have been able to learn helpful tools that work.

To my son Wil Jr. and daughter-in-law Elandra my daughter Cindy and son-in-law Frank, who are actively navigating the ever-challenging work that is required to establish a long-lasting and loving relationship.

To my five granddaughters ranging in age from 11 to 20: Nylah, Joi, Layla, Leah, and Ayanna: this book will hopefully provide them with tools helpful in decreasing some of the stress, hurt, miscommunications, or roadblocks that often prevent acquaintances from becoming long-lasting and loving relationship partners.

6 Keys to a Lasting Relationship:
Volume 1
— A Resource for Making it Work

Contents

6 Keys to a Lasting Relationship:
Volume 1
– A Resource for Making it Work

Contents – cont'd

6 Keys to a Lasting Relationship:
Volume 1
– A Resource for Making it Work

Deciding to work on it or walk away

If you find yourself in the position of trying to decide rather to work on saving a relationship or to walk away, this is a workbook designed to bring clarity to the process.

I suggest that any major decisions in life should be considered very carefully over a period of time before arriving at a conclusion. "Be Still," You can see and hear more clearly!!

6 Keys to a Lasting Relationship, Volume 1, A Resource for Making it Work was designed as quick resource for working through relationship issue as well as a tool for building individual self-confidence.

6 Keys to a Lasting Relationship:
Volume 1
– A Resource for Making it Work

ACKNOWLEDGMENTS

The journey to the compilation of this book has been filled with people to whom I will be forever grateful. Of course, there is no way for me to list all the names of people that have actively provided ideas, research, and encouragement, as well as those that have contributed to the emotional content upon which this book is grounded.

To my dearly departed father, the honorable Reverend Stephen S. Waller, thank you for introducing me to the love of God from whence cometh my health, my strength, my wisdom, and the solid rock upon which I stand. Thank you for showing by example, that neither social struggle nor life's peaks and valleys can tear apart a committed relationship emanating from an open, honest, and authentic foundation.

I also want to acknowledge my saintly mother who resides with the angles, Mary L. Braxton-Waller, also known as Mary Sue. Thank you for being a shining example of grace in times of peace and adversity. Because of the example that you modeled in overcoming relationship challenges, I learned tools that I have used in my own relationship and that I can now share with others working toward sustaining long-term loving relationships.

6 Keys to a Lasting Relationship:
Volume 1
– A Resource for Making it Work

Acknowledgements – cont'd

To my former classmates at Norfolk State University and LaSalle University, thank you for the many conversations debating the validity of traditional marriage, monogamy, and nuances of newer forms of couplings and partnerships.

To my friends, clinical staff, and colleagues at the Freire Charter Middle School and the Center for Families and Relationships, I cannot begin to express how grateful I am for the opportunity grow stronger at my skills and crafts, while helping to improve the lives of clients and their support systems.

6 Keys to a Lasting Relationship:
Volume 1
– A Resource for Making it Work

Inspirations for Book

Research study after

research study has concluded that human-

beings are social by nature.

Human-beings are animals that seek

Connections and relationships

to others where they live, work, and play.

6 Keys to a Lasting Relationship: Volume 1 – A Resource for Making it Work

Inspirations for Book - cont'd

In a poem pinned in 1623 by

English author John Donne, it is

written that:

No man is an Island

Entire of itself,

Every man is a piece of the continent,

A part of the main"

This book "6 Keys to a Lasting Relationship"

speaks to man-kinds

need for connections and how to develop

and maintain

long-lasting and loving relationships.

6 Keys to a Lasting Relationship:
Volume 1
– A Resource for Making it Work

What's Your Role?

As we live and grow, we develop all types of relationships along our journey. Mere short-term acquaintances typically will not require maintenance. However, monthly, weekly, or even daily, relationships will likely require work and maintenance if they are to be successful over a period of time.

Work, school, social, and intimate relationships are the most common relationships that require purposeful work and maintenance. Having the ability to recognize your role in maintaining any relationship will be vital in achieving the rewards of such relationships.

I encourage self-inspection and self-reflection as the first step in the process. Working on ones' self and being willing to acknowledge flaws as well as accept recognition for ones' gifts is a must.

6 Keys to a Lasting Relationship:
Volume 1
– A Resource for Making it Work

Types of Relationships

Acquaintance

Boss-Employee

Classmate

Co-Worker/ Colleague

Friends

Friends w/benefits

Intimate

Parent-Child

Romantic

Sibling

There are many types of relationships. This book "6 Keys to a Lasting Relationship" focuses primarily on romantic committed relationships, even though the 6 keys can be broadly applied to any of the other relationships.

Other handbooks specifically addressing keys to success for any of the other listed relationships, as well as how to manage specific Emotional Disorders will be coming soon.

6 Keys to a Lasting Relationship:
Volume 1
– A Resource for Making it Work

6 Keys to a Lasting Relationship: List

1. Awareness
2. Believing
3. Communication
4. Digging Deep
5. Emptying the blame jar
6. Fixing self, first

6 Keys to a Lasting Relationship:
Volume 1
– A Resource for Making it Work

KEY #1

AWARENESS

6 Keys to a Lasting Relationship: Volume 1 – A Resource for Making it Work

Key # 1 – Awareness

Key #1 - Awareness: the state of knowing. Consciousness, the ability to identify, clarity

Knowing the real you, acknowledging the actual truths about yourself; being genuine with yourself will allow you to present an authentic person to a relationship partner; Identify positive and negative beliefs, behaviors and characteristics of yourself; form a clear list of strengths to build confidence in yourself; focus on weaknesses that can be improved or eliminated.

A clear and strong sense of your authentic self makes for a better relationship partner. This is also true when you make a commitment and take the necessary steps to address and meet your own needs and wants.

Working alone, with a support group, or a professional proficient in your area of need, the outcome is most often a whole, complete, and confident you. Research has shown that confident people are better able to maintain stronger and longer lasting relationships.

Consciousness – a state or sense of awareness or sensitivity to a particular issue or situation.

6 Keys to a Lasting Relationship:
Volume 1
– A Resource for Making it Work

Key # 1 – Awareness – cont'd

When you become conscious or aware of who you are as a person, your positives and negatives, strengths and weaknesses, wants, needs, and goals, it is much easier to set goals and a direction for the future.

Bringing a conscious and aware individual into a relationship increases the potential for a long- lasting loving relationship.

One of the major elements in doing the work to becoming whole is being sincere and honest with yourself. It is important to have the **ability to identify** and separate negative and positive stories you, and those around you, have told you about the truth about who you are. Mom, dad, siblings, teachers, friends, acquaintances, and co-workers, all have different experiences with you.

Therefore, the perception of you will vary. Hence, the things they tell you about who you will also differ.

- **Clarity** – having clarity means that you are clear about who you are and know what your needs, boundaries, and expectations are. Being unclear is often a culprit in poor communication issues which can handicap the success of any long-term relationship.

6 Keys to a Lasting Relationship:
Volume 1
– A Resource for Making it Work

Key # 1 – Awareness – cont'd

- When you have no confusion about who you are, what you need and want, your strengths and weaknesses, goals, expectations, and boundaries, you will have a much better ability to communicate to a partner clearly and precisely.

6 Keys to a Lasting Relationship:
Volume 1
– A Resource for Making it Work

Do Your Work
Key 1 - Awareness

List:

- **3 Truths you know about yourself:**

- **3 negatives that you are aware or conscious of that need work:**

6 Keys to a Lasting Relationship:
Volume 1
– A Resource for Making it Work

Do Your Work

Key # 1 – Awareness – cont'd

- 3 perceptions others have of or that you have been told about your-self that you believe are inaccurate:

- 3 things that you know you cannot tolerate that would be a relationship deal breaker for you:

6 Keys to a Lasting Relationship:
Volume 1
– A Resource for Making it Work

Author's Note
Key # 1 – Awareness

As a result of doing your work in the key #1 awareness section, I would like to review what you have learned about yourself:

Were you able to list 3 truths, 3 negatives, 3 inaccurate perceptions, and 3 things that would be relationship dealbreakers for you? If you did, great job! If you didn't, perhaps there were not 3 issues in each question that needs addressing, which is fine.

But if, internally you know there are more issues that needed to be listed and you did not do so, perhaps this is an indication of areas that are most problematic, due to denial or avoidance. These areas are likely areas that may require the most attention.

Knowing yourself, becoming aware and conscious of the truths, perceptions, and negatives about yourself is the first step in building self-confidence. Now that you know these things, how do you feel about yourself? Are you pleased, or do you wish to change either of these characteristics about yourself?

6 Keys to a Lasting Relationship:
Volume 1
– A Resource for Making it Work

<u>Author's Note</u>
<u>Key # 1 – Awareness, cont'd</u>

It is my hope that you will use this book as a tool to get to know yourself better. I hope that you will work on things that you perhaps would not have brought into your daily consciousness if you were not doing the exercises in this book.

6 Keys to a Lasting Relationship:
Volume 1
– A Resource for Making it Work

KEY #2

BELIEVING

6 Keys to a Lasting Relationship:
Volume 1
– A Resource for Making it Work

Key # 2 – Believing

Key # 2 - Believing – when you *accept something to be true.* having *confidence* in something, accepting something to be *real; accepting something to be sincere and genuine.*

- *Accepting something to be true* – believing something to be in total alignment with your sense of reality or the facts as you know them to be. Your truth may or may not be consistent with someone else's idea of the truth about you. When in a relationship, one of the keys to making it last is being able to present your true self and to allow your partner to present their truth, even when it does not align with your own.

TIP: Remember, beliefs are often direct products of past experiences, current experiences, and/or generational beliefs. Your relationship partner's experiences will be different than yours.

Seek information- Seeking answers and understanding of what one believes is totally different than subscribing to suspicions and accusations, with no supportive evidence. Behaviors just described can be very damaging to any relationship.

6 Keys to a Lasting Relationship:
Volume 1
– A Resource for Making it Work

Key # 2 – Believing – cont'd

Settlement of situations and events from your past will positively impact your current attitudes and behaviors. When in a relationship you should seek to learn, understand, and respect your own life's experiences before attempting to understand and resolve your partners' issues.

- Having *confidence* in something – convicted to the faith and belief in oneself or something; a high level of trust in oneself, a person, or an outcome of a situation.

  Have you heard the old saying "you complete me" or "you make me whole" well I am sorry to tell you that both statements are myths. **One person cannot complete or make another person whole.**

  When an individual makes a commitment and takes necessary steps to address and meet their own needs and wants, alone or with the aid of support groups or appropriate professionals, the outcome is most often a whole, complete, and *confident* individual. Research has shown that confident individuals have typically been able to maintain stronger and longer-lasting relationships.

6 Keys to a Lasting Relationship:
Volume 1
– A Resource for Making it Work

Key # 2 – Believing – cont'd

Accepting something as *real* – pertaining to fact or actuality; not imaginary or necessarily ideal.

Have you ever talked with someone and thought to yourself, "man, they must be living in an alternate reality?" The things that they say and the things they believe, seem so foreign or unbelievable to you.

Remember that I have cautioned you that your set of life experiences and perceptions differ from anyone else's, your siblings and even your partner. Individuals experiencing the same event at the same time may well perceive the experience differently. Hence, your reality is unique to you.

The ability to communicate some of your life experiences and your resulting reality, to your partner, should be helpful in building a more solid understanding of who you are as a person, leading to a better and longer-lasting relationship.

- Accepting something to be ***sincere and genuine*** –to be sincere is to be honest; not falsified or made up; to be genuine is to be actual; true; not counterfeit.

6 Keys to a Lasting Relationship:
Volume 1
– A Resource for Making it Work

Key # 2 – Believing – cont'd

One of the major elements in doing your work to becoming whole is being sincere and honest with yourself.

Identifying and separating negative and positive stories you and those around you have told you about the truth about who you are, is equally important.

As mentioned earlier, Mom, dad, siblings, teachers, friends, acquaintances, and coworkers, all have different experiences of you. Therefore, the perception of you will vary. Hence, the things they tell you and others about who you are will also vary.

Knowing the real you, acknowledging the actual truths about yourself, and being genuine with yourself will allow you to present an authentic person to a relationship.

TIP: Identify positive and negative beliefs, behaviors and characteristics of yourself; form a clear list of strengths to build confidence in yourself and focus on weaknesses that can be improved or eliminated. A clear and strong sense of your authentic self makes for a better relationship partner.

6 Keys to a Lasting Relationship:
Volume 1
– A Resource for Making it Work

It Takes Two

There is always more than one person in a relationship. In order to achieve a successful relationship, there must be clear and understandable communication of want each person needs or expects from the relationship.

Communication is an important Key in any successful relationship. Assuming that the other person automatically knows or understands your wants or needs is a recipe for trouble.

Each person in the relationship should communicate things that they find to be very important to them. Verbal communication is very good, how-ever I encourage written or other documented form of communication in addition to verbal, as to avoid the proverbial, "That's not what I said" later on down the road.

6 Keys to a Lasting Relationship:
Volume 1
– A Resource for Making it Work

Do Your Work
Key # 2 – Believing

List:

- **3 things that people believe about you that are not true:**

- **3 things about yourself that make you feel confident**

6 Keys to a Lasting Relationship:
Volume 1
– A Resource for Making it Work

Do Your Work
Key # 2 – Believing – cont'd

- **3 things about yourself that you may not necessarily like, but that you can accept:**

- **3 people that you feel you can be sincere and genuine with:**

6 Keys to a Lasting Relationship: Volume 1 – A Resource for Making it Work

Author's Note
Key # 2 – Believing

As a result of doing your work in the key #2 Believing section, I would like to review what you have learned about yourself:

Were you able to list 3 truths, 3 areas of confidence, 3 things that are real to you, and 3 people who you feel you can be genuine and sincere with? If you did, great job! If you didn't, spend a little more time on each question until you are able to do so. I believe that everyone should be able to list at least 3 answers to each of these questions.

Once you have acknowledged areas of truth, reality, and sincerity, you are that much closer to having the ability to discern the difference between truth, reality, and things that change from person to person or situation to situation.

Having truth, reality, and sincerity surrounding you, encourages confidence in yourself and your surroundings. Knowing who you are, what's real and what's open to interpretation, cuts down on confusion on what to believe and what not to believe.

6 Keys to a Lasting Relationship:
Volume 1
– A Resource for Making it Work

Author's Note
Key # 2 – Believing, cont'd

Now that you are more aware of truths about yourself, you have a better sense of your true self. Do you have belief in yourself?

How are you feeling about yourself? Is your confidence building? Have you noticed that awareness and consciousness results in clarity and confidence?

It is my hope that you will use this book as a tool to become aware of issues you may be having and to get clarity on what to believe about yourself. Use it to work on things that you may not have brought into your daily consciousness if you were not doing the exercises in this book.

6 Keys to a Lasting Relationship:
Volume 1
– A Resource for Making it Work

KEY #3

COMMUNICATION

6 Keys to a Lasting Relationship: Volume 1 – A Resource for Making it Work

Key #3 – Communication

Key # 3 - Communication – the act of exchanging thoughts, messages, or information using eye contact, *body language, technical devices, or verbally.*

- *Eye contact* – making direct eye contact can indicate confidence, while looking down or away gives the impression of lack of confidence; professionals often use direct eye contact or lack of eye contact as a way to assess whether a person is telling the truth or not or if they are shy or depressed.

- **Body language** – assessing a person's physical or emotional state using their gestures, postures, or facial expressions. Body language is usually an automatic and uncontrolled set of actions and reactions.

- **Technological devices** – no tech device is required to communicate with oneself; your mind and body send messages to each other all day every day. Practice in tuning into these messages is recommended to help you become better at recognizing and interpreting these messages.

6 Keys to a Lasting Relationship:
Volume 1
– A Resource for Making it Work

Key #3 – Communication – cont'd

- When communicating with the many relationships around you, considerations must be taken-into-account, for age, gender, educational level, ethnic background, and personal life, which all contribute to a variety of different preferences, devices, and communication styles.

Verbal communication – verbal and oral communication is the use of words to speak your feelings, thoughts, and emotions. The inflections (variations in pitch or tone) of how you deliver your communication can change whether it is received, negatively or positively.

TIP: The act of exchanging thoughts, messages, or information using eye contact, body language, technological devices, or verbally is one a major element in a long-lasting relationship.

Communication is typically not a solitary exchange, rather an interaction between two or more entities in which each hears and knowledges the other, no matter rather they agree with one another or not.

6 Keys to a Lasting Relationship:
Volume 1
– A Resource for Making it Work

Key #3 – Communication – cont'd

Reflective Listening (paraphrasing or restating What *a* person has said to you, while being sensitive to the emotions attached to it).

Practicing **Reflective Listening** usually has a reciprocal effect. When someone feels heard or validated, they are more prone to listen and validate the other person. It is not necessary to invalidate someone else's perspective in-order to present your own.

Using a calm, non-elevated tone of voice is likely to be heard and received. In contrast, elevated, loud, or aggressive tone is likely to be tuned out or met with an equally loud, aggressive, or confrontational tone. Loud, aggressive, and monopolizing talk time comes off as threatening and is likely to be met with resistance.

Having regularly scheduled meetings to review items of concern that may be impacting your relationship is a good idea.

It is suggested to maintain a journal with dated entries, listing your concerns, and to have that journal available in your regularly scheduled meeting. Have your partner jot down your concerns and their responses to your concerns; this practice will confirm understanding of your concerns and their commitment to address them.

6 Keys to a Lasting Relationship:
Volume 1
– A Resource for Making it Work

Key #3 – Communication – cont'd

TIP: remember to use "I" statements during your meeting while presenting your concerns: using "you" statements, more-often-than-not, puts your partner on the defensive and can sabotage the goal of a positive outcome.

6 Keys to a Lasting Relationship:
Volume 1
– A Resource for Making it Work

Do Your Work
Key # 3 – Communication

List:

- **3 situations in which you find it awkward to make eye contact**

- **3 words that best describes your typical body language**

6 Keys to a Lasting Relationship:
Volume 1
– A Resource for Making it Work

Do Your Work
Key # 3 – Communication – cont'd

- **3 ways that you believe your tech device has or can hurt your relationships**

- **3 things that you think you could do to improve your communication skills**

6 Keys to a Lasting Relationship: Volume 1 – A Resource for Making it Work

Author's Note
Key # 3 - Communication

As a result of doing your work in the key # 3 communication section, I would like to review what you have learned about yourself:

Were you able to list 3 situations in which it is difficult for you to make eye contact, 3 body language habits that you exhibit (negative or positive), 3 occasions in which your digital devices hurt your relationship, and 3 things that you feel you could do to improve your communication skills? If you did, great job! If you didn't, it's alright as long as you feel that you have listed all the situations that are relevant to the questions.

If you listed 3 situations in which you find it difficult to make eye contact, it may signal that you may be shy, have a lack of confidence, or perhaps suffering from social anxiety or other mental health condition. I encourage you to identify which fits you best.

All of these conditions can be managed with proper attention. Social Anxiety is the most severe condition of the 3, but it also can be managed with proper attention.

6 Keys to a Lasting Relationship:
Volume 1
— A Resource for Making it Work

<u>Author's Note</u>
<u>Key # 3 – Communication, cont'd</u>

What are the 3 body language habits you listed? Does your non-verbal communication gestures express closeness, openness, happiness, sadness, or anxiety? Body language can tell the outside world a lot about you without you opening your mouth.

Digital devices are a part of the fabric of everyday life. From Siri, Alexa, cell phones, desktops, laptops, home monitoring devices, to baby cams and pet cams, digital devices are all around us all day every day.

Significant Clinical Research has not yet come in that helps to determine the benefits or negative impacts of these devices. However, early data does suggest that the decreasing amount of eye-to-eye human contact and interactions has already shown to have a negative impact on intimate relationships. How have digital devices impacted your life?

6 Keys to a Lasting Relationship: Volume 1 – A Resource for Making it Work

Author's Note
Key # 3 – Communication, cont'd

Closely related to the question about digital devices is the question about ways that you feel you could improve your communication skills. Limiting use of digital devices is optimal in improving interpersonal or intimate communications. Listening, understanding, and consideration of the other are other big tasks to master on the road to good communication.

It is my hope that you will use this book as a tool to learn methods and techniques that will help you to improve your ability to make eye contact, exhibit positive body language, limit use of digital devices, communicate better with your partner, and to work on things that you otherwise may not have brought into your daily consciousness .

6 Keys to a Lasting Relationship:
Volume 1
– A Resource for Making it Work

KEY #4

EMPTYING THE BLAME JAR

6 Keys to a Lasting Relationship: Volume 1 – A Resource for Making it Work

Key # 4 – Emptying the Blame Jar

Key # 4 - Blame – to hold responsible for an error, negative behavior, or action

- **Emptying the blame jar -** when events, big or small, happen in your life, it is natural to store away feelings, reactions, and emotions associated with those events. You may attribute positive memories to the person(s) responsible for the positive events. However, when the event is negative, assigning blame to the person(s) responsible, many find it necessary to process the blame, with the responsible person(s), before storing it away.

- *Negative events* in your life that are stored away before they are processed, have the potential to fester over time and become the basis of an emotional disorder requiring professional help to resolve, in much the same way that any unattended disease, injury, or medical condition would.

- How do you *process the blame*? If possible, discuss what happened with the person(s) involved. If each person is able to be heard by the other, this will go a long way toward reaching an understanding. However, if talking it over with one-another, tuning the other out, or either party is unavailable or unwilling

6 Keys to a Lasting Relationship:
Volume 1
– A Resource for Making it Work

Key # 4 – Emptying the Blame Jar, cont'd

to communicate, then perhaps a mediator or mental health therapist is indicated.

Finding out and communicating each persons' understanding of the core or underlying situation or issue that led to the negative event is a necessary step that must be taken before you can begin to *eliminate or reduce the level of blame*. Do not simply look for what the other person(s) did wrong, but also do some self-reflection to find out what words, actions, and behaviors of yours may have contributed to the negative event.

If there is regret or remorse from both parties for their words, actions, or behaviors, then moving to the next step in the process is in order.

After agreeing on what happened, why it happened, and how each person contributed, the final step in the process of emptying the blame jar would then be discussing what changes in behavior or actions will be taken by each party in-order to prevent that negative event from recurring

6 Keys to a Lasting Relationship:
Volume 1
– A Resource for Making it Work

<u>Do Your Work</u>
<u>Key # 4 – Emptying the Blame Jar</u>

List:

- **3 traumatic or negative events that you have experienced that you have not been able to forget:**

- **3 steps that you have taken to help you get past the traumatic or negative experiences:**

6 Keys to a Lasting Relationship:
Volume 1
– A Resource for Making it Work

Do Your Work
Key # 4 – Emptying the Blame Jar –cont'd

- **3 people that you feel are responsible for what happened to you:**

- **3 things that you think you could do to reduce or Eliminate the blame you feel toward them:**

6 Keys to a Lasting Relationship: Volume 1 – A Resource for Making it Work

Author's Note
Key # 4 – Emptying the Blame Jar

As a result of doing your work in the key # 4 Emptying the Blame Jar section, I would like to review what you have learned about yourself:

Were you able to list 3 traumatic or negative events that you have experienced that you have not been able to forget, 3 steps that you have taken to help you get past the traumatic or negative experiences, 3 people that you feel are responsible for what happened to you, and 3 things that you think you could do to reduce or eliminate the blame you feel toward them?

If you did, great job! If you didn't, Keep working! It is important to acknowledge the trauma to begin the healing process. Please list all situations that are relevant to the questions.

Let's take a look at what you listed as traumatic or negative events that you cannot forget. When was it; how old were you; did it happen to you or did you witness it; if you cannot forget it, have you ever sought help to get past it?

6 Keys to a Lasting Relationship:
Volume 1
– A Resource for Making it Work

Author's Note
Key # 4 – Emptying the Blame Jar – cont'd

Traumatic and negative events often lead to symptoms of anger issues, anxiety, or other mental health conditions, which can be managed with proper attention.

With reference to the 3 traumatic or negative events that you listed above, if you stated that you have not been able to forget it, the next question asked for 3 actions you have taken to help decrease or eliminate the memories. Have you shared it with a family member, close friend, teacher, church elder, school counselor, or therapist?

The longer you hold it in means you are choosing to hold on to the pain, anxiety, and anger associated with the trauma.

Who were the 3 people you listed that you feel were in any way responsible for what happened? Where are they now; do you still see them; would you like to confront them about what happened?

The sooner you are able to confront the experience and the people involved with it, the sooner you will be able to begin the process of healing.

6 Keys to a Lasting Relationship:
Volume 1
– A Resource for Making it Work

It is necessary to heal from any traumatic or negative event that you have experienced because any relationship that you are involved with, will be impacted by your experiences.

What did you list as 3 things or ways that you can begin to forgive the person(s) that you feel are responsible? Acknowledge what happened; make a decision to forgive; tell someone of your intention to forgive which will help you to be accountable to your commitment; and finally write in your journal a date that you hope to put the experience behind you. Forgiveness opens the heart up for healthier relationships.

It is my hope that you will use this book as a tool to learn methods and techniques that will help you to acknowledge and get past traumatic or negative events, and to contact the people that you feel are responsible to work together to reduce, eliminate, and forgive any associated blame.

Awareness, believing, communicating, reducing blame with forgiveness, are all areas to work on that you may not have brought into your daily consciousness if you were not doing the exercises in this book.

6 Keys to a Lasting Relationship:
Volume 1
– A Resource for Making it Work

KEY #5

DIGGING DEEP

6 Keys to a Lasting Relationship: Volume 1 – A Resource for Making it Work

Key # 5 – Digging Deep

Key #5 - Digging Deep – digging deep refers to doing the work that is necessary to maintain a long-lasting relationship; compromising; forgiving; letting go; standing up.

It may seem easy, fun, and exciting to be in a relationship during the honeymoon phrase (generally 6 months to a year), but eventually after you begin to become settled in, being on your best behavior to make a good impression is no longer a priority, and the routine of everyday life sets in.

This is the time when you become more aware of practices, habits, and attitudes that, if left unchecked, could present problems in the relationship. This is also the time when work should begin if your goal is a long-lasting relationship.

- *Compromise* – to settle differences by relaxing or giving in on a circumstance or point-of-view in return for concessions by your partner.

The most common areas that couples run into conflicts that require a commitment or compromise to resolve are cleanliness, spending habits, parenting style, the balance between social

6 Keys to a Lasting Relationship:
Volume 1
− A Resource for Making it Work

Key # 5 – Digging Deep – cont'd

time and family time, differences in love language, and career goals and motivations.

If both people are relatively neat, no problem; if one is a **slob** and the other is a **neat-freak,** work, concessions, and compromise is required from both to resolve the conflict.

Listing household chores that each person is good at and then sharing and agreeing to commit to share the less pleasing responsibilities would go a long way in resolving the neatness and cleanliness issues. In today's society with both parents working outside of the house, it is necessary for both parents and children over the age of ten to share equally in the division of the household upkeep. Mom and Wife is not the maid!!

- **Spending** is a huge issue in-that whether there is a single income, several incomes are combined, or if assigned financial responsibilities from separate incomes, is the arrangement, how well the spending and payments are managed, determines the need for compromise on budget restructuring.

6 Keys to a Lasting Relationship: Volume 1 – A Resource for Making it Work

Key # 5 – Digging Deep – cont'd

It is suggested that all monthly bills such as mortgage, rent, utilities, insurances, food, entertainment expenses, savings accounts, and other expenditures not listed, be managed monthly on a budget spread sheet. A special savings or slush account should be maintained to handle any instance of outside or emergency expenditures.

- *Parenting styles* frequently cause conflict in relationships and require continued attention and adjustments. Some parents tend to be permissive, allowing their children free reign: some are authoritarian, insisting on strict obedience from the children, no-matter what.

Contrastingly, some parents are more authoritative in nature: practicing warm, loving, reasoning, and open communication behaviors.

Clinical research has found that authoritative parenting style has been proven to result in more positive and healthy outcomes for children; From the time newborns become a part of the family, to the time they leave as young adults, each parents' style should be reviewed, adjusted, and compromises agreed upon.

6 Keys to a Lasting Relationship:
Volume 1
– A Resource for Making it Work

Key # 5 – Digging Deep – cont'd

The ***balance between social time and family time*** presents as one of the most frequently cited conflicts that couples have expressed in a clinical setting.

When trying to find a workable balance between family time and social outings, simply having time together as a family should be the higher priority. With a calendar in hand, work and school schedules should be plugged in first every evening, after work, school, homework, and dinner, at least one to two hours per day for staying alert and aware of positive as well as negative situations that may exist with either member of the family).

Setting aside at least two weekends for family time should be a priority. One weekend date night every six weeks should be scheduled for the couple. One to two weekends per month may then be available for social events or activities.

Differences in love language **- love language is defined as the ways in which a person shows their love and dedication to another person. It is quite likely that two people in a relationship have different love languages because a person's love language is informed by multiple factors such as nature, nurture, life experience, trauma, and personality.**

6 Keys to a Lasting Relationship: Volume 1 – A Resource for Making it Work

Key # 5 – Digging Deep – cont'd

The most common love languages in intimate relationships are expressed in the form of sexual intimacy, giving gifts, words of affirmation, serving their partner, physical touch, and spending quality time.

Some people who are uncomfortable verbally expressing their love, devotion, and affection for some-one, find it much easier to buy **gifts** that should surely indicate the depths of their affection.

Some shower their partner with praise, compliments and other **affirming** claims, without directly expressing how highly they are thought of.

It is human nature to seek validation and approval, which is why the praise, compliments, and other words of affirmation from your partner, makes you feel loved and more connected.

Still others play **the servant**, waiting on their partner hand and foot; you must know I love you if I am willing to do all of this for you.
Giving and doing for others, tends to have positive long-term effects: from lowering blood pressure, feelings of contentment and happiness and even increasing life expectancy.

6 Keys to a Lasting Relationship:
Volume 1
– A Resource for Making it Work

Key # 5 – Digging Deep – cont'd

Having the willingness to be of service to your partner will likely have a reciprocal affect in the relationship because being altruistic (a selfless concern and willingness to do for others) can be contagious.

Research has revealed that touching is beneficial to physiological and psychological well-being by lowering heart rates and blood pressure as well increasing oxytocin levels (oxytocin is a hormone that promotes feelings of love, social bonding, and well-being).

Finally, many feel loved while spending relaxed, comfortable, **quality time** with their partner. whether you take a weekend trip together, work on a special DIY project, play board games, or simply net flicks and chill, relaxed time together yields positive results for the relationship.

Since love language is informed by multiple factors such as nature, nurture, life experience, trauma, and personality, no matter what your preferred love language is, understanding that just because you may feel more comfortable with a love language does not mean that your partner feels most loved with that same language.

6 Keys to a Lasting Relationship:
Volume 1
– A Resource for Making it Work

Key # 5 – Digging Deep – cont'd

If your goal is a long-lasting, loving relationship, practicing your partner's preferred love language for their benefit is a sure bet that they will feel so loved by you that they are more likely to practice your preferred love language for your benefit.

- *Forgiving* – to forgive, is to free oneself from the feelings of resentment, or desire to punish someone else for offensive words, action, or behavior.

  Forgiveness can be very difficult, and increasingly so with the severity of the offense. Should I forgive him/her? How long can I keep this anger inside? Can I trust him/her again? What if it happens again? These are all typical questions asked after a person has been hurt or offended.

6 Keys to a Lasting Relationship:
Volume 1
– A Resource for Making it Work

Key # 5 – Digging Deep – cont'd

When considering forgiveness, it is a good idea to remember that no one is perfect, not even you; list the pros and cons of the relationship; consider the frequency of the offensive words, action, or behavior; clearly communicate your hurt and need for the offensive words, action, or behavior never to occur again; and finally make a fair and unemotional decision (never make any kind of decision when your emotions are high); once the decision is made, stick to your guns.

- *Letting go* – when you let go, you release yourself from the negative and hurtful feelings and emotions; you reclaim your freedom and feelings of liberation.

If you have decided to forgive, it is then on you to let go of the hurt, anger, and resentment. If you say you will forgive, but continue to punish your partner through negative words, actions, and behaviors, you yourself may well be pushing your partner right back to those offensive behaviors that hurt you in the first place.

6 Keys to a Lasting Relationship:
Volume 1
– A Resource for Making it Work

Key # 5 – Digging Deep – cont'd

Standing up – standing up in reference to relationships, means that you are emotionally strong enough to communicate your needs, wants, and desires for personal safety, security, stability, and satisfaction.

Often times when an individual feels a lack of confidence in their own self-worth or abilities, they conform with or go along with whatever is happening in the relationship, even negative behaviors that make them feel even more unsafe, insecure, unstable, or unsatisfied.

It is important to standup for yourself, if you hope for any chance for a stable, long-lasting and loving relationship. Acknowledging your shortcomings, working on them, and seeking professional help for emotional goals that you cannot control, manage, or achieve on your own, are a few of the first steps necessary to take to achieve those goals.

6 Keys to a Lasting Relationship:
Volume 1
– A Resource for Making it Work

Review

How are you doing?

What have you learned about yourself?

Are you motivated to become self-reflective?

Have you identified areas that may require
professional assistance?

6 Keys to a Lasting Relationship:
Volume 1
– A Resource for Making it Work

Do Your Work
Key # 5 – Digging Deep

List:

- 3 compromises that you are willing to make in the next last 6 months that will improve your relationship with self or with your intimate relationship.

- 3 people that you can forgive for wrongs you believe have been perpetuated against you.

6 Keys to a Lasting Relationship:
Volume 1
– A Resource for Making it Work

Do Your Work
Key # 5 – Digging Deep – cont'd

- 3 things or hurts that continue to come up when you are upset, that you are willing to make a commitment to work through and let go of.

- 3 things that you want to stand-up to and take charge of but may need some help to do it.

6 Keys to a Lasting Relationship: Volume 1 – A Resource for Making it Work

Author's Note
Key # 5 – Digging Deep

As a result of doing your work in the key # 5 Digging Deep section, I would like to review what you have learned about yourself:

Were you able to list 3 compromises you are willing to make to improve your relationship with self, or with your intimate relationship; 3 people that you can forgive; 3 things or hurts that continue to come up when you are upset; and 3 things that you want to stand-up to and take charge of. If you did, great job! If you didn't, does that mean there are no areas that need work? This is the time to come clean and work toward claiming the relationship that you want.

What did you list as 3 ways you are willing to compromise in your relationship? Some of the common areas that couples struggle with and have to compromise in order to resolve the issues are rules for disagreements or verbal fighting, frequency of sex, finances, balancing family and social activities, and responsibilities to parents. When you agree to a compromise, it is recommended that it is put in writing and initialed by both parties to insure understanding in the future.

6 Keys to a Lasting Relationship: Volume 1 – A Resource for Making it Work

Author's Note
Key # 5 – Digging Deep – cont'd

If you can recall, forgiveness was addressed in Key # 4 in the section about reducing and eliminating blame, and it is addressed again here in Key # 5.

-

It is recommended that you make a commitment to yourself to work on or correct any negative impressions of self, prior to committing to a long-term relationship.

Your Realities – your perception of self and your realities are closely linked, but they are not the same. As previously explained, your perception of self is informed by your reaction to things seen, heard, and experienced by you, as well as the things that you have been told by those in your immediate environment. Your reaction to these experiences informs your perceptions in relationship to the people, events, and circumstances in your life.

The distinction between your perception and your reality is that your reality consists of facts that are informed not by your reaction to things seen, heard, or experienced, but by data that is true, real, actual, and does not change based on perceptions or stories told.

6 Keys to a Lasting Relationship:
Volume 1
– A Resource for Making it Work

Author's Note
Key # 5 – Digging Deep – cont'd

It may be helpful to seek a third party, perhaps a close family member, a long-time friend, or a professional therapist, to help you sort out actual facts and what are simply your perceptions of the facts. Understanding the real you, makes you a better candidate for a long- lasting relationship.

Having the ability to forgive may not be easy to come by, but it is worth the work because is not only freeing for the person being forgiven, but it also opens the heart for inner peace, decreases depression and anxiety, and reduces episodes of anger related to the event.

What did you list as 3 occasions that to be you have been hurt and still find it difficult to let it go? Some important ideas to consider that may help in the process of forgiving and letting go, are 1, remember that no one is perfect, 2, consider your contribution to the hurtful event, and 3, acknowledge your hurt and accept your partners assurance that it will not happen again.

6 Keys to a Lasting Relationship:
Volume 1
– A Resource for Making it Work

Author's Note
Key # 5 – Digging Deep – cont'd

If you have been successful in compromising, forgiving, and letting go of the hurt, then you should have no problem standing up to and taking charge of your emotional health.

It is my hope that you will use this book as a tool to learn methods and techniques that will help you compromise, improve your relationship with your intimate partner, forgive the wrongs you feel have been perpetrated against you, and release yourself from rehashing hurtful events of the past.

6 Keys to a Lasting Relationship:
Volume 1
– A Resource for Making it Work

KEY #6

FIXING SELF FIRST

6 Keys to a Lasting Relationship:
Volume 1
– A Resource for Making it Work

Key # 6 – Fixing Self, First

Key # 6 - Fixing Self, first – entails exploring your perception of self, your realities, your perceived presentation of self, and your distorted beliefs about self; you will also begin acquiring knowledge, tools, and skills to help you build self-esteem, actualization, presentation, and self-regulation.

The perception you have of yourself is most often put in place by the time you are 5 years old. It is formed by how the people in your home react to you and the stories they tell you about yourself.

Perception of self – the way you view yourself in different contextual environments (physically, intellectually, socially, etc.) and your reaction to that view.

You may see yourself as short or tall, smart or intellectually challenged, socially awkward or the bell of the ball; no matter how you perceive yourself, the view is often incongruent (not in-line with) the facts of the situation, how others view you, as well as the fact that perception is always relative to others that you are comparing yourself to.

6 Keys to a Lasting Relationship:
Volume 1
– A Resource for Making it Work

Key # 6 – Fixing Self, First – cont'd

Whatever perception you have of yourself is the same perception you will take into a relationship. If you have a negative perception of self, your partner will eventually accept or adopt that same perception of you.

Your Perceived Presentation of Self – the way that you believe that the essence of you, from appearance, speech, and aura, to your behavior, presents or conveys an image or information about you to others, often times, how you think you are presenting yourself to others, is not the way others are receiving you.

One group may receive you in one way, while another group may receive you in a totally contrasting way.

Do you present a different side of yourself when you are with specific individuals or groups? feel compelled to put on a good face in public, that is different than your private persona? Does social and cultural expectations sway your behavior.

6 Keys to a Lasting Relationship:
Volume 1
– A Resource for Making it Work

Key # 6 – Fixing Self, First – cont'd

Your goal should be to evaluate your truths, strengths, weaknesses, and distorted beliefs about yourself. At the end of the process, accept, adopt, and strengthen the traits that feel most authentic and natural to your inner self.

With this self-awareness, begin to build self-esteem self-confidence, and self-love that can be presented consistently, both publicly and privately. Self-confidence has consistently proven to be
one of the most frequent elements of a long-lasting relationship.

Beliefs About Self - beliefs are facts and/or opinions about self; distorted beliefs are false, misleading, or adverse representations of the truth. From the time you are born, you are told messages about your appearance, weight, behavior, intelligence, and other ways to describe you.

Typically, these messages are received, believed, and accepted to be true because they are given to you by the people closest to you.

6 Keys to a Lasting Relationship:
Volume 1
– A Resource for Making it Work

Key # 6 – Fixing Self, First – cont'd

During the onset of puberty, because of the physical, emotional, and hormonal changes that take place during this phrase of life, it is normal human behavior to begin to examine yourself both internally and externally.

People surrounding you may be able to offer their impressions of who you are externally, but you are the expert on your thoughts, feelings, and emotions internally. When there is an obvious difference in the perception of you and the real you, anxiety is often the result.

If you are able to identify the discrepancies distortions between your public presentation and the real you, you may be able to dispel or correct the false perceptions and put forth a more truthful representation of who you are as a person.

6 Keys to a Lasting Relationship:
Volume 1
– A Resource for Making it Work

Key # 6 – Fixing Self, First – cont'd

Self-presentation – any *actions and behaviors* you display that conveys or infers information or an image of who you are as a person.

Self-esteem – how you *think* of yourself, either in a negative or positive way.

Self-regulation – your ability to *control or change* your behavior or responses

Self-actualization – to reach the full potential of your desires, talents, and abilities

6 Keys to a Lasting Relationship:
Volume 1
– A Resource for Making it Work

<u>Do Your Work</u>
<u>Key # 6 – Fixing Self First</u>

List:

- **3 positive things about yourself (high self- esteem)**

- **3 ways that you hope you present yourself publicly (self-presentation).**

6 Keys to a Lasting Relationship:
Volume 1
– A Resource for Making it Work

Do Your Work
Key # 6 – Fixing Self First – cont'd

- 3 situations or behaviors that you feel you need to do better
  at controlling or managing (self-regulation).

- 3 needs, dreams, or goals that you have achieved that
  have helped you move in a positive direction (self-
  actualization).

6 Keys to a Lasting Relationship:
Volume 1
– A Resource for Making it Work

Do Your Work
Key #6 – Fixing Self First – cont'd

If you are able to achieve levels of self-presentation, self-esteem, self-regulation, and self-actualization that feels good, natural, and authentic to you, your probability of being successful in developing and maintaining a long lasting and loving relationship increase exponentially.

6 Keys to a Lasting Relationship:
Volume 1
– A Resource for Making it Work

Author's Note
Key # 6 – Fixing Self, First

As a result of doing your work in the key # 6 Fixing Self, First, section, I would like to review what you have learned about yourself:

Were you able to list 3 positive things about yourself (high self-esteem), 3 ways that you hope you present yourself publicly (self-presentation), 3 situations or behaviors that you feel you need to do better at controlling or managing (self-regulation), and 3 needs, dreams, or goals that you have achieved that have helped you move in a positive direction (self-actualization). If you did, great job! If you didn't, Keep working. Fixing Self is a goal that only you can set for yourself. The rewards of doing the work can last a life-time.

Thinking of yourself in positive terms (high self-esteem) is a must before you can hope to have a successful relationship.

Research has shown that how you feel about yourself is what you teach others feel about you. When you are positive about yourself, you will share that positivity with your partner. Alternatively, when you feel negative about yourself, you bring that negativity into your relationship.

6 Keys to a Lasting Relationship: Volume 1 – A Resource for Making it Work

Author's Note
Key # 6 – Fixing Self, First, cont'd

TIP: repeating a personal mantra at the beginning of each day is very helpful in building positive self-esteem; every morning before beginning your day, repeat to yourself 3 times: I was created to be Uniquely me!!

How do you think others see you? What is your public persona (self-presentation)? Do you care? Research shows that confident people or people with high self-esteem worry less about their public persona, but people with low self-esteem, constantly seek approval, acceptance, or validation of their public image.

TIP: if you fix the parts of self that you are not happy with, then the true-self and the public-self can merge and you will become a whole, content self, privately and publicly.

What did you list as the 3 situations or behaviors that you feel you need to do better at controlling or managing (self-regulation)? Self-regulation, better known as self-control, can be achieved in 3 steps.

.

6 Keys to a Lasting Relationship:
Volume 1
– A Resource for Making it Work

<u>Author's Note</u>
<u>Key # 6 – Fixing Self, First, cont'd</u>

Common areas that people suggest that they need help in self-regulation are, dieting, exercising, studying, anger management, and emotional regulation (i.e. stress, anxiety, depression). Pick one behavior to work on, tackling too many issues at the same time decreases the likelihood of success; the 3 steps are:

TIP: (1) <u>Commitment</u> – commit to what you want and create practical plans to achieve it, (2) <u>Monitor</u> your progress – keep track of your progress on regularly predetermined intervals, and (3) <u>Stick to it</u> - any goals that you set will involve change, and any change involves apprehension; don't allow any apprehension de-rail your goals.

What did you list as 3 needs, dreams, or goals that you have already achieved, that have helped you move in a positive direction in life (self-actualization)?

Needs, dreams, and goals can be very small, from making the perfect omelet or cleaning your room, to very big, like getting your dream job or buying a new home. The positive feelings of joy and satisfaction that come with achievement gets you one step closer to self-actualization.

6 Keys to a Lasting Relationship:
Volume 1
– A Resource for Making it Work

Author's Note
Key # 6 – Fixing Self, First, cont'd

TIP: Set small achievable goals, once achieved, set a new more challenging one, with practical time goals (record all changes, big and small, positive and negative).

If you are able to achieve levels of self-presentation, self-esteem, self-regulation, and self-actualization that feels good, natural, and authentic to you, your probability of being successful in developing and maintaining a long lasting and loving relationship increase exponentially.

6 Keys to a Lasting Relationship: Volume 1
– A Resource for Making it Work

Mantras for "6 Keys"

"How you relate to the relationships

around you,

Is informed by the relationships

that formed you"

Barbara Waller-Johnson, BS, MA. MFT

6 Keys to a Lasting Relationship:
Volume 1
– A Resource for Making it Work

Books Coming Soon:

"6 Keys to Managing Anxiety -

Navigating Coronavirus,

Isolation, and Uncertainty"

"The Un-United States of –

2 Americas"

6 Keys to a Lasting Relationship:
Volume 1
– A Resource for Making it Work

Advice & Blogs:

For sensible insights into relationships:

read my weekly **Blog**:

https://gbarb0015.wixsite.com/mysitemyblog

Also:

Relationship and Life advice is

available for a fee of $ 5.00 at:

Relationship Rescue – Help Is Here

– Ask Ms. Barb:

https://relationshiprescuerefresh.com

6 Keys to a Lasting Relationship:
Volume 1
– A Resource for Making it Work

Good Luck

Made in the USA
Middletown, DE
21 August 2020

15914458R00052